What is Prompt Engineering and why is it important in 2025?

In 2025, mastering artificial intelligence won't be just for programmers. Prompt engineering is the art of communicating with tools like ChatGPT, Gemini, or MidJourney using precise instructions to get incredible results without writing code.

• Everyday example:

"Tell me about the weather" → Generic response.

"Summarize the weather in Madrid for tomorrow in 3 lines, with emojis and tips for leaving the house" → Useful and personalized response.

In a world where AI is in your email, your work, and even your refrigerator, knowing how to write prompts (instructions) will be the most profitable skill of the future.

"This book is for you if..."

✔ You have no technical experience but want to use AI like a pro.

✔ You get frustrated when tools don't understand what you're asking.

✔ You are a student, entrepreneur, marketer, or someone curious about saving hours of work.

✔ You think "only engineers" can take advantage of AI (spoiler: not true).

How to Use This Book

• Practical Exercises: At the end of each chapter, challenges to apply what you've learned (e.g., "Write a prompt that generates a vegan meal plan in seconds").

• Downloadable Templates: Prompts ready to copy and paste into your favorite tools.

• 2025 Secrets: Updated techniques for next-generation AI models.

Basic Concepts

In this chapter, we'll break down the fundamentals of prompt engineering so you understand how to interact with AI effectively, without the need for advanced technical knowledge.

What are prompts and how do they work in AI?

A prompt is an instruction, question, or text that you give to an AI to generate a response. Think of it as giving clear orders to a smart assistant.

How a prompt works:

1. **Input**: You write a text (e.g., "Give me 3 ideas to post on LinkedIn about digital marketing").

2. **Processing**: The AI analyzes the text, interprets it, and looks for patterns in its trained data.

3. **Output**: It generates a response based on what it "learned" during its training.

Example of improvement with prompt engineering:

"Talk about artificial intelligence" → *Generic and long response.*

"Explain artificial intelligence in 3 lines to a 10-year-old" → Clear and tailored response.

Differences between **ChatGPT**, **Gemini**, **Claude**, and other models (2025)

Not all AIs respond the same. Each model has its strengths:

Developer Model Best for Use Case

ChatGPT: OpenAI Creative text, brainstorming, writing "Write a short poem about the ocean"

Gemini: Google DeepMind Precise searches, Google integration: "Summarize this scientific article into key points"

Claude: Anthropic Logical reasoning, long documents "Analyze this contract and highlight risks"

Llama 3 Meta (Facebook) Open-source, customization "Generate Python code for a scraper"

Tip 2025:

- Use ChatGPT for creativity.

- Use Gemini if you need up-to-date data.

- Use Claude for detailed analysis.

Key Vocabulary in Prompt Engineering

1. Tokens

- These are "chunks" of words that the AI processes.

- Example: "Hello" = 1 token, "Artificial Intelligence" = 2-3 tokens.

- Important: Some models have token limits (e.g., 4,096 in GPT-4).

2. Temperature

- Controls creativity vs. AI Accuracy:

 Low (0.2): More predictable and technical answers.

 High (0.8-1.0): More original (but risky) answers.

3. Few-Shot Prompting

- Provide examples in the prompt to guide the AI:

Copy

Download

Example of a few-shot prompt:

"Translate these phrases into French:

- 'Hello' → 'Bonjour'

- 'Thank you' → 'Merci'

Now translate: 'How are you?'"

4. System Prompt (Hidden Instruction)

- "Invisible" message that configures the AI's behavior:

 Example: "You are an expert historian. Respond in an academic tone."

Practical Exercise

Objective: Use a prompt with few-shot learning to have the AI complete a task.

Instructions:

Copy

Download

"Examples of blog titles:

- 'How to learn Python in 30 days'

- 'Quick guide to digital marketing 2025'

Now, generate 3 similar titles about ,artificial intelligence for business .

Business Prompts (Save Work Hours)

1. Business Idea Generation

Prompt:

"Act like a startup consultant. Give me 5 innovative digital business ideas for 2025, with less than $1,000 initial investment. Include a monetization model for each one."

Example output:

"1) Virtual Assistant for Freelancers: Use AI to manage emails, invoices, and reminders. Monetization: Monthly subscription. 2) 'AI for Local Businesses' Course...

2. Persuasive Emails (Sales or Networking)

Prompt: "Write a short email (max. 150 words) to sell a web design service to small restaurants. Use a friendly tone and highlight 'increasing online reservations' as a key benefit."

Example output:

"Hi [Name], Did you know that 70% of customers choose restaurants with fast and easy-to-use websites? At [Your Company], we create mobile-optimized sites that help..."

3. Quick Market Analysis

Prompt:

"Analyze consumer trends in [your industry] for 2025. Give me 3 opportunities and 3 risks, in bulleted list format."

Creative Prompts (Viral Content & Design)

1. Reel/TikTok Scripts

Prompt:

"Generate 3 Reel script ideas (15-30 seconds) on 'AI productivity.' Include opening hook, transition, and CTA (e.g., 'Which will you try? Let me know in the comments!')."

Example:

"Hook: 'Do you spend hours organizing your day? AI does it in 2 seconds.' → Transition: (Split screen: you annotating vs. AI app screen.)" → CTA: Leave your questions below!

2. Brand Name Brainstorming

Prompt:

"I am a sustainable clothing brand for young people. Give me 10 creative names in Spanish or English, that include words like 'eco', 'green', or 'future'. Explain the meaning of each one."

Example:

"**1) EcoVibe**: Combines ecology and lifestyle.

2) GreenThread: Sustainable threads with impact..."

3. Brief for Designers (MidJourney/DALL-E)

Prompt for images:

"Generate a minimalist logo for a coffee shop called 'Nómada'. Use earth tones, a cup icon with a travel map, and clean sans-serif typography. Style: vector."

Professional Prompt Template (Responsive)

Copy

Download

"Act as [role: expert in X]. My goal is [clear objective].

- Output format: [list/table/paragraph].

- Tones: [professional/fun/urgent].

- Avoid: [technical terms/unsourced data].

- Include: [examples/statistics 2025].

Rules for Writing Effective Prompts

In this chapter, you'll learn a scientific method for creating prompts that generate useful, precise, and tailored answers. We introduce the CLEAR formula, comparative examples, and critical mistakes to avoid.

The CLEAR Framework: Your Formula for Mastering AI

Exclusive method based on analysis of 500+ successful prompts by 2025

1. **Context**

What it is: The "statement of purpose" that defines the role, audience, and objective.

Example:

"Talk about digital marketing."

"You are a marketing consultant with 10 years of experience. Explain how to use Instagram Reels to sell online courses to Latinx entrepreneurs."

2. **Length**

What it is: Specifying length avoids short or unnecessarily long answers.

Example:

"Tell me about blockchain."

"Explain blockchain in 1 paragraph (max. 5 lines) for a beginner."

3. **Examples**

What it is: Providing samples guides the desired style/tone (few-shot prompting).

Example:

Copy

Download

"Translate into English while maintaining a formal tone:

- 'We appreciate your preference' → 'We appreciate your trust.'

Now translate: 'Our team is at your disposal.'"

4. Adjust

What it is: Technical parameters such as temperature or output formats.

Example:

"Generate company names."

"Generate 10 AI startup names. Temperature: 0.7. Format: numbered list with brief description."

5. Refine

What it is: Iterate based on initial results.

Technique 2025: Use "Critique this prompt and suggest improvements: [your prompt]" for self-debugging.

Bad vs. Good (Detailed Analysis)

Ineffective Prompt Category Optimized Prompt (CLEAR) Why It Works

Writing "Write an essay." "Write a 300-word essay on the impact of AI on employment (2025). Academic tone, 3 sources cited in APA." Clear context, defined length, specific format.

Design "Draw a logo." "Generate a vector logo for a coffee shop called 'Solar'. Use yellow #FFD700 and black, a stylized sun icon, and a modern sans-serif typeface."* Precise visual and technical details.

Programming "Help with Python." "Fix this Python code that scrapes Twitter (ERROR on line 15). Explain the solution in steps." Technical context and type of explicit help.

Common Mistakes (and How to Fix Them)

1. Ambiguity

Problem: "Do something creative." → The AI doesn't understand the objective.

Solution: "Generate 3 ideas for an urban mural in Madrid that combines AI and flamenco. Style: surreal."

2. Oversaturation

Problem: "Write a viral LinkedIn post about leadership with emojis, statistics, Jobs quotes, and 5 hashtags. Inspiring but also educational." → Too many contradictory instructions.

Solution: "Write a LinkedIn post (200 words) about Steve Jobs' leadership lessons for startups. Motivational nonsense. Include 1. relevant statistic and 2 hashtags (#Leadership #Startups)."

3. Ignoring AI Feedback

Problem: Not adjusting the prompt after mediocre answers.

Technique 2025: Use "The previous answer was too [X]. Rewrite with more [Y] and less [Z]."

Downloadable CLEAR Template

(Include in book as a graphic resource)

Copy

Download

CONTEXT: [Role + Objective + Audience]

LENGTH: [Length or duration]

EXAMPLES: [Style/tone samples]

ADJUST: [Temperature, format, constraints]

REFINE: [Instruction to iterate]

__Practice Exercise__

Goal: Turn this ineffective prompt into a CLEAR one:

"Tell me how to make money."

Suggested Solution:

Copy

Download

"Act like a savvy digital business entrepreneur (2025). Give me 3 realistic strategies to earn $500/month from home, with concrete examples and initial requirements. Format: bulleted list."

Case Study: Transforming Results with Prompt Engineering

Real Case: TechB2B (SaaS Startup)

Goal: Improve lead generation through AI-powered automated emails.

Phase 1: Ineffective Prompt (Wasting Time and Opportunities)

Copy

Download

"Write an email to sell our project management software."

Problem Result:

▸ Generic email (287 words)

▸ Zero personalization

▸ Open rate: 14% (vs. 21% industry)

CLEAR Error Analysis:

1. Lack of context (doesn't mention customer pain points)

2. Lack of length (redundant text)

3. Lack of examples (doesn't use proven persuasive language)

_____

Stage 2: Optimized Prompt (CLEAR Formula)

Copy

Download

"You are a senior copywriter specializing in B2B SaaS.

- **Objective**: Email for CTOs of companies with 50-200 employees experiencing project delays.

- **Length**: Max. 150 words.

- **Example pitch**: 'Does your team waste 12 hours/week in unproductive meetings?'

- Adjustments: Include one statistic and a clear CTA.

- Refine: If the text sounds too technical, add an everyday analogy."

Results (30 days):

Open rate: 34% (+143%)

Click-through rate: 11% (vs. 5% previously)

3 demos purchased (value: $15,000 USD)

Key Lessons

1. Specificity Attracts the Right Audience

• **Before**: "Management software" → Too broad.

• **After**: "Solution for CTOs with remote teams" → Clear niche.

2. Data Builds Trust

• Original prompt ignored statistics.

• **CLEAR version included: "68% of SaaS projects fail due to poor coordination (Gartner 2024)."**

3. Refinement is Key

TechB2B iterated 3 times:

1. **First version**: Too long.

2. **Second**: Unclear CTA.

3. **Third**: Perfect balance.

_____

Template for Your Case Study

(Adaptable to any industry)

Copy

Download

INITIAL PROBLEM:

[Description of the failed prompt]

CLEAR ANALYSIS:

Missing context: _____

- Technical errors: _____

OPTIMIZED PROMPT:

[Use CLEAR structure]

SUCCESS METRICS:

[Before] vs. [After] + % improvement

LESSONS:

1. _____

2. _____

_____

Practical Exercise: Apply CLEAR to Your Industry

Instructions:

1. Choose a real-life case (e.g., emails, content generation, customer service).

2. Write the worst possible prompt for that task.

3. Convert it into a CLEAR prompt using the template.

Example (Healthcare):

"Answer patients who ask for prices."

"You are a dental clinic assistant. Answer questions about whitening prices in 2-3 lines, with an empathetic tone and a link to the personalized quote form. Example: 'We understand the investment is significant...'"

Advanced Case Studies: E-Commerce & Education

E-Commerce Case: Increasing Conversions on Shopify

Company: ModaÉtica (sustainable clothing)

Problem: Generic product descriptions (2.1% conversion rate).

Prompt Failed

Copy

Download

"Describe this organic cotton dress."

Result:

"Organic cotton dress. Available in sizes S-XL. Colors: blue, black."

Prompt CLEAR Optimized

Copy

Download

You are a senior copywriter in sustainable fashion for eco-conscious millennials.

- **Context**: GOTS cotton midi dress, made in Spain.

- **Length**: 120 words (3 paragraphs).

- Example of tone: 'This isn't just a dress, it's your vote for a better planet.'

- Adjustments: Include:

1. Ethical benefits (e.g., "2500L of water saved vs. conventional").

2. Care instructions as a list.

3. Emotional call-to-action (#DressWithPurpose)."

Results (30 days):

Conversion: 5.8% (+176%)

Time on page: +40 seconds

Returns: -12% (better description = clear expectations)

Key Lesson:

"In e-commerce, prompts should sell experiences, not technical specifications."

Education Case Study: Personalizing Content for Virtual Classrooms

Institution: AcademiaTech (AI courses for teachers)

Problem: Highly technical materials (32% dropout rate in lesson 3).

Failed Prompt

Copy

Download

"Explain machine learning to teachers."

Outcome: Text with equations and terms like "gradient descent."

Optimized CLEAR Prompt

Copy

Download

"You are an expert educator in digital literacy.

- **Context**: Explain what machine learning is to high school teachers without a technical background.

- **Length**: 1 paragraph (max. 5 lines) + everyday analogy.

- **Example**: 'ML is like when Netflix learns your tastes...'

- *Adjustments:*

1. Avoid technical jargon.

2. Include one example applicable to classrooms (e.g., plagiarism detection).

3. Final reflective question ('How could you use it in your classes?')"

Results:

Retention: 89% completed the lesson (+57%)

Positive feedback: 4.8/5 stars

Recommendations: +22% enrollment

Key Lesson:

"In education, prompt engineering should prioritize clarity over technical precision."

Ready-to-Use Templates

E-Commerce Template (Product Descriptions)

Copy

Download

"You are a [niche] copywriter for [audience].

- **Product**: [Name + key features].

- **Tone**: [e.g., inspirational/urgent/practical].

- **Include**:

1. [Emotional benefit].

2. [Sustainable/ethical fact].

3. [Specific CTA: e.g., 'Complete your look with...']"

Education Template (Explaining Complex Concepts)

Copy

Download

"You are an educator specializing in [topic] for [academic level].

- **Concept to explain**: [_____].

- **Avoid**: [Technical terms like _____].

- **Requirements**:

1. Everyday analogy.

2. Example applied to [student context].

3. Suggested visual (e.g., 'Imagine that...')."

Exercise: Diagnose and Repair

Faulty prompt (e-commerce):

"Write an Instagram post about these shoes."

Your mission:

1. Identify 3 CLEAR errors.

2. Rewrite using the template.

Expert Solution:

Copy

Download

"You are a community manager for a vegan shoe brand. Create an Instagram post (caption + 3 hashtags) that:

1. Uses storytelling ('These shoes were born when...').

2. Highlights that 2 trees are planted for every purchase.

3. **CTA**: 'Ready to walk toward a sustainable future? [Link in bio]'

Case Studies by Industry:

Professional structure with:

• Detailed subsections by vertical

• Real-life examples 2025

• Downloadable templates (exclusive lead magnet)

Digital Marketing: Creative Automation

1. Emails that Convert (CLEAR Template)

Prompt:

Copy

Download

"You are a performance copywriter for [industry]. Create a nurturing email for [target audience] that:

- Opens with a painful question (e.g., 'Tired of [specific problem]?')

- Include a shocking statistic (e.g., '68% of...')

- **Clear CTA**: 'Schedule your demo today → [link]'

Format: Max. 180 words, [urgent/empathetic] tone."

Case Study:

• **Company**: CRM SaaS

• **Result**: +32% openers vs. Generic emails

2. Viral Posts for Social Media

LinkedIn Prompt:

Copy

Download

"Generate 3 viral post ideas about [2025 trend] for [professional profile]. Requirements:

- First-person hook ('I made this mistake...')

- Numbered list with actionable tips

- Engagement question ('Have you tried this? Tell me ↓')

Example pitch: @garyvee."

Lead Magnet:

Education: AI as a Pedagogical Assistant

1. Curriculum Design

Prompt:

Copy

Download

"You are an AI pedagogue. Design a 4-week curriculum on [topic] for [level]. Include:

1. SMART objectives per week

2. Interactive activities (e.g., 'Discussion: How would you apply [concept] in [real-life context]?')

3. Non-traditional assessment metrics

Format: Table with columns 'Week', 'Content', 'Activity'."

Case Study:

• **Institution**: Coding Bootcamp

• **Result**: Reduced planning time by 60%

2. Custom Exam Generation

Prompt:

Copy

Download

"Create an exam on [topic] with:

- 5 multiple-choice questions (medium difficulty)

- 2 case studies (e.g., 'Analyze this dataset and...')

- Evaluation rubric with levels from 'Excellent' to 'Needs Improvement'

Exclude: Theoretical questions from memory."

Lead Magnet:

➔ *Educator Kit 2025: "Prompt Pack for Smart Classrooms" (Includes prompts for feedback, gamification, and more).*

Business: Express Analytics with AI

1. Executive Reports in Minutes

Prompt:

Copy

Download

"Analyze this Q2 2025 sales dataset and generate an executive report (1 page) with:

1. 3 key insights (e.g., 'Category X grew 120% in segment Y')

2. Suggested chart (type + variables)

3. Actionable recommendation

Tone: Managerial, no technical jargon."

Case Study:

• **Company**: Multinational retailer

• **Time saved**: 8 hours → 15 minutes

2. Meeting Summaries with AI

Prompt:

Copy

Download

"Summarize this meeting transcript into:

- 3 key agreements (format: 'WHAT' + 'WHO' + 'WHEN')

- 2 points of contention

- 1 open question for the next session

Exclude: Irrelevant information."

Lead Magnet:

➔ *"CEO Pack: 15 Prompts to Automate Your Business" (Includes SWOT, pitch decks, and more).*

Daily Life: AI as a Personal Assistant

1. Smart Meal Planning

Prompt:

Copy

Download

"Generate a weekly meal plan for:

- 2 adults and 1 child

- **Diet**: Mediterranean

- **Restrictions**: No seafood, max prep time 30 min

Format: Shopping list + recipes in 1 click (links)."

. Hyper-Personalized Travel Itineraries

Prompt:

Copy

Download

"Act as a travel planner for [destination]. Create a 3-day itinerary with:

- **Mornings**: Cultural activities

- **Afternoons**: Relaxation/local hidden gems

- **Evenings**: Restaurants [vegan/romantic/etc.]

Include: Maps optimized by area and budget."

Lead Magnet:

Performance Metrics with Prompt Engineering

Why Metrics Matter

By 2025, leading companies will measure the ROI of their prompts with 3 key KPIs:

1. Time saved (**efficiency**)

2. Improved conversion (**commercial impact**)

3. Perceived quality (**human feedback**)

Industry Benchmark (**Real Data 2025**)

E-Commerce

Metric Before AI With Optimized Prompt Improves

Time spent on descriptions 45 min/product 6 min/product -87%

Product conversion 2.1% 5.8% +176%

Returns 23% 11% -52%

Case Highlight:

- *ModaÉtica increased cross-sells by 34% with prompts like:*

"Recommend 2 products that match [item purchased]. Format: Instagram carousel with direct links."

Digital Education

Metric Before AI With Optimized Prompt Improved

Lesson planning time 8h/week 2h/week -75%

Lesson retention 32% 89% +178%

Student satisfaction 3.2/5 4.8/5 +50%

Proven technique:

- *Use of "Explain [concept] like a Twitter thread for Gen-Z" → +62% in engagement.*

B2B Business

Metric Before AI With Optimized Prompt Improved

Reporting speed 12h/report 1.5h/report -87.5%

Unnecessary meetings 6/week 2/week -66%

Qualified leads 15/month 42/month +180%

Star Prompt:

"Analyze these 50 prospecting emails and classify them as: 'Hot' (need a demo), 'Warm' (educate), 'Cold'. Justify in 1 sentence."

How to Measure Your Own Results

1. A/B Prompt Testing

• **Group A**: Generic Prompt (e.g., "Summarize this article")

• **Group B**: CLEAR Prompt (e.g., "Summarize this article in 3 bullets for CEOs, highlighting financial implications")

• **Key Metric**: Usage Rate/Engagement with the Exit

2. Quality Surveys

Include at the end of interactions:

"Was this response helpful? [1-5] What was missing?"

▶ **Example**: AI legal assistant improved accuracy from 68% to 91% after iterating prompts based on feedback.

3. Time vs. Value

Task Without AI With Raw AI With Prompt Engineering

Create blog content 4h 1h (generic) 25 min (editorial quality)

Exclusive Lead Magnet

"PRO Metrics Kit":

• Notion template to track improvements by prompt

• 10 formulas ready for Google Sheets (e.g., "% time savings = ((old hours - new hours)/old hours)100")

• Extended case study: How FinTechBoost scaled to €1M ARR using these KPIs

Practical Exercise: Turn Data into Action

Your current results:

• **Prompt used: "_____"**

• **Metric to improve:** _____ (e.g., time, conversion, satisfaction)

Redesign the prompt by applying:

1. CLEAR Specificity

2. Technical parameters (temperature=0.3 for accuracy)

3. Success stories (use the benchmark table above).

Free and Paid Tools:

Which Tool Do You REALLY Need?

Quick Guide by User Type

Profile Best Free Option Best Premium Option Why?

Entrepreneurs ChatGPT 3.5 ChatGPT Plus ($20/month) 24/7 support for emails, ideas, and customer service

Students Gemini Free Claude Pro ($25/month) Summarizes long PDFs and explains complex concepts

Creatives Microsoft Copilot (Free) MidJourney ($10/month) Generates images from text prompts

Data Analysts Perplexity Free ChatGPT Team ($25/user) Extracts data from Excel/PDFs and creates charts

Everyday example:

"If you just want help writing social media posts, ChatGPT 3.5 is sufficient. But if you need to analyze 100-page legal contracts, Claude Pro is worth it."

2025 Comparison: *ChatGPT Plus vs. Gemini Advanced vs. Claude Pro*

Features: **ChatGPT Plus** ($20) **Gemini Advanced** ($22) **Claude Pro** ($25)

Message Limit: 40/hour 60/hour 100/hour

Files: Yes (PDF, Excel) Google Drive Only: Yes (up to 10MB)

Web Search: Manual (activate) Automatic: No

Key Strength: Creativity Up-to-date data Logical Reasoning

CEO Tip:

• **Choose ChatGPT Plus** if: You want more "human" and creative responses.

• **Choose Gemini if**: You work with Gmail/Google Docs and need real-time information.

• **Choose Claude if**: You accurately analyze long documents.

_____

Must-Have Extensions (Free)

1. AIPRM for Chrome

• **What it does**: Gives you preconfigured 1-click prompts for marketing, SEO, and sales.

• **Real-world example**:

  Built-in prompt: "Generate a viral **TikTok** script about [product]" → Ready in 20 seconds.

2. WebChatGPT

• What it does: Adds automatic web search to **ChatGPT**.

• Use cases:

"Compare iPhone 15 prices at Amazon, Best Buy, and Walmart" → Gives you up-to-date data.

3. Merlin

• What it does: Use **ChatGPT** on any website (e.g., summarize Twitter threads).

• **Example**:

"Summarize this Forbes article into 3 key points" (no copy/paste).

Pro Tip: Combine Tools

Example workflow (no code):

1. Research with Perplexity (current data).

2. Write with ChatGPT Plus (persuasive tone).

3. Check for errors with Grammarly (grammar).

4. Design images with Canva Magic Write (AI + design).

Time Savings: 3 hours → 35 minutes.

Exclusive Lead Magnet

"Super Toolkit 2025":

• Downloadable list with 50+ preconfigured prompts for AIPRM.

• Video tutorial (15 min): "How to set up Merlin in 2 steps."

• Notion template to compare the costs/benefits of each tool.

Exercise: Choose Your Ideal Stack

Instructions:

1. Write down your top 3 tasks with AI (e.g., writing emails, analyzing data).

2. Select 1 free and 1 paid tool from the comparison table.

3. Try them this week and record:

o Time saved: _____

o Quality vs. before: [1-5]

Tool-Specific Prompts (Quick Start)

Goal:

Learn to "speak" to each AI like a practical expert, without technical jargon.

ChatGPT-4 (OpenAI) – The Creative

Strength: Original ideas, persuasive writing.

Prompt examples:

1. For Entrepreneurs

"Act like a startup consultant. Give me 3 low-cost strategies to validate [business idea] in 2 weeks. Format: actionable steps + metrics to track."

2. For Viral Content

"Write a Twitter thread (12 tweets) explaining [complex concept, e.g., blockchain] with everyday analogies. Use emojis every 3 tweets. Tone: Playful but precise."

3. For Daily Life

"Create a 21-day plan to develop [habit, e.g., meditation]. Include:

• Daily routine (max. 10 min)

• Progress checklist

• 3 motivational quotes (one per week)."

Gemini Advanced (Google) – The Researcher

Strength: Up-to-date data, Google integration.

Example prompts:

1. For Business

"Compare the average prices of [product, e.g., air fryers] on Amazon, Walmart, and Target in 2025. Organize in a table with: brand, price, average rating, and link."

2. For Students

"Summarize this academic article [paste URL] into 3 key points. Then, generate 5 multiple-choice questions to assess comprehension (answers included)."

3. For Travel

"Plan a 5-day itinerary in [city] for [profile, e.g., family with kids]. Include:

• 1 morning activity (cultural)

• 1 local restaurant (medium budget)

• 1 safety tip per day."

Claude Pro (Anthropic) – The Analyst

Strength: Processing long documents, logical reasoning.

Example prompts:

1. For Lawyers/Accountants

"Review this [type] contract and highlight in red:

- Risky clauses

- Critical deadlines

- Ambiguous terms.

Format: table with page # + comment."

2. For Writers

"Analyze this chapter of my novel [paste text]. Suggest:

- 3 pacing improvements

- 1 character to develop further

- 1 powerful visual metaphor for the key scene."

3. For Mental Health

"You are a cognitive-behavioral therapist. Give me 3 exercises to manage [situation, e.g., workplace anxiety]. Include:

- Duration

- Materials needed

- Research supporting this (APA format)."

MidJourney v6 – The Designer

Strength: Hyperrealistic images.

Prompt Examples:

1. For E-Commerce

"Generate an image of [product, e.g., eco-friendly watch] in a forest at sunrise. Style: professional photography, natural light, 8K details. Include sustainable packaging in the scene."

2. For Social Media

"Create a meme about [topic, e.g., remote work]. Style: cartoon illustration, pastel color palette, text: 'When AI understands your prompts better than your boss.'

Universal Template for Any Tool

"Act as [role]. I need [clear objective].

" - Output Format: _____

- Tone: _____

- Avoid: _____

- Include: _____

(Tool-specific: add parameters like 'temperature=0.5' or '—v 6' for MidJourney here)."

Additional Lead Magnet

"50 Tool-Specific Prompts":

• Downloadable PDF with prompts for **ChatGPT**, **Gemini**, **Claude**, and more.

• **Include**:

o Email templates for each platform

o Prompts for data analysis (Excel/Google Sheets)

o Visual style guide in MidJourney

Exercise: Adapt Your Prompts

Original prompt: "*Tell me about artificial intelligence.*"

Your challenge:

1. For **ChatGPT**: Turn it into a storytelling prompt.

2. For **Gemini**: Ask for updated data.

3. For **Claude**: Request a critical analysis.

Solutions:

• **ChatGPT**: "Tell the The history of AI as if it were a children's story. Includes one character and one moral lesson.

• **Gemini**: "Show the three leading AI companies in 2025, with their market value and latest innovation."

• **Claude**: "Analyze the ethical risks of AI in 500 words. Cite two recent controversial cases."

Final CEO Tip

"Each AI is like an employee with distinct superpowers:

• **ChatGPT** is your star copywriter.

• **Gemini** is your research assistant.

• **Claude** is your trusted analyst.

Use them as a team."

Advanced Prompts for Specialized Tools:

Focus:

✔ Master lesser-known but powerful tools

✔ Practical examples for each user profile

✔ Clear comparisons: When to use them vs. ChatGPT/Gemini?

Perplexity AI – The Data Detective

Forte: Real-time searches with cited sources. Ideal for researchers and journalists.

Prompt Examples:

1. For Journalists:

"Find the 3 latest statistics on [topic, e.g., AI adoption in hospitals] in 2025. Official sources only (WHO, governments). Answer in journalistic format: 'According to X study...' with links."

2. For Investors:

"Compare the growth of NVIDIA vs. AMD over the past 6 months. Include:

• % stock market growth

• Latest product launch

• 1 potential risk per company."

3. For Academics:

"Find peer-reviewed studies from 2024-2025 that demonstrate [hypothesis, e.g., 'AI improves medical diagnoses']. Summarize methodology and key findings in 1 paragraph per study."

Pro Tip:

Use "filetype:pdf" in your prompts to search only for academic papers.

Llama 3 (Meta) — The Customizable Assistant

Forte: Open-source, ideal for technical projects and experiments.

Prompt Examples:

1. For Developers:

"Generate Python code for a Telegram bot that:

• Answers weather questions using an API

• Saves interactions to SQLite

• Includes comments every 5 lines."

2. For Content Creators:

"Write a 5-minute YouTube script explaining [technical concept] to beginners. Structure:

• Everyday problem (example)

• Simple explanation

• Visual demo (text in parentheses for editing)."

3. For Local Businesses:

"Create a custom prompt for my bakery that:

- Generates daily Instagram posts

- Uses a warm tone and emojis

- Automatically includes weekly promotions."

Key Settings:

Always add "--temperature 0.3"* for precise technical answers.

Comparison Table: When to Use Each One?

Need Best Prompt Tool Example

Updated data with Perplexity sources "Which countries will lead in AI regulation by 2025? Government sources."

Open Source Projects Llama 3 "Generate a README.md for my financial analysis repository."

Creative Brainstorming ChatGPT-4 "10 ideas for AI fitness app names."

Long Document Analysis Claude Pro "Summarize this 50-page PDF into 10 bullet points."

Powerful Extensions and Combos

1. Perplexity + Notion AI

Flow:

1. Search data in Perplexity.

2. Use "Organize this information in a Notion table with columns: Source, Date, Finding."

2. Llama 3 + Zapier

Automation:

"When you receive an email with an 'urgent request,' have Llama 3 generate a response and send it via Gmail."

Lead Magnet: "Niche Tools Guide 2025"

Includes:

- 15 prompts for Jasper (commercial copywriting)

- 10 templates for ElevenLabs (AI voice for podcasts)

- Video tutorial: How to install Llama 3 on your PC

Book Offer:

"Download the Complete Pack: [QR Code]"

Exercise: Create Your Custom Stack

Step 1: Choose your most repetitive task (e.g., researching competitors).

Step 2: Combine 2 tools:

- **Example**: Perplexity (data) + ChatGPT (presentation).

Step 3: Design a bridge prompt:

"Take this data from Perplexity and turn it into a 1-page executive report with suggested charts."

Expert Tips 2025

1. For entrepreneurs: Use Perplexity to validate business ideas with real data before investing.

2. For students: Llama 3 is ideal for translating technical notes into simple language.

3. Common mistake: Not adjusting the temperature in Llama 3 (use 0.2-0.5 for accuracy, 0.7+ for creativity).

Audio/Video Tools, Automation, and Costs

Professional Approach for Non-Technical Users:

✔ Ready-to-Copy/Paste Examples

✔ Visual Comparison Charts

✔ Real-Life Workflows

AI Audio/Video Tools (With Specific Prompts)

1. ElevenLabs (Realistic Voice)

Prompt for Podcasters:

"Convert this script to audio with:

• Voice: Male, warm tone ('educational podcast' style)

• Speed: 110%

• Dramatic pauses at [insert key phrases]

• Output format: MP3 192kbps"

Real Case: Save 80% vs. human voice talent for audiobooks.

2. Runway ML (AI Video Editing)

Prompt for reels:

"Edit this raw video (30 seconds) by adding:

• Animated subtitles (typewriter style)

• Zoom morph transition every 5 seconds

• Background music: Soft electronica (bpm: 100)

• Export in 1080p for Instagram"

Advanced example:

"Generate an explainer video using these 3 slides. Style: Kinetic Typography. Duration: 45 seconds."

3. Murf AI (Multilingual Voices)

E-learning **Prompt**:

"Create a narration in neutral Spanish and English (UK) for this course. Requirements:

• Emphasis on technical terms

• 2 seconds of silence between paragraphs

• Mark timestamps for editing"

Automation with Zapier/IFTTT (Flows + Prompts)

1. Automated Responses to Clients

Flow: Gmail → ChatGPT → Slack

Zapier **Prompt**:

"When an email arrives with the subject 'URGENT', generate a 2-line response:

1. Receipt confirmation

2. Estimated resolution time (e.g., 24-48 hours)

2. Social Media Auto-Posting

Flow: Google Sheets → Canva → LinkedIn

IFTTT **Prompt**:

"When a row is added to the 'ContentCalendar' sheet, create a post with:

• 'MinimalistBlue' Canva Template

• Text: [Column B] + hashtags #[Column C]

• Publish on Wednesdays at 9 AM

3. Smart Meeting Backup

Flow: Zoom → Claude → Notion

Prompt:

"Transcribe this meeting and organize in Notion:

1. Agreements (table with responsible party/date)

2. Pending items

3. Mentioned resources

API Cost Comparison 2025

Tool	Basic Plan	Limits	Cost 1M Tokens	Best For
OpenAI GPT-4 Turbo	$20/month	40 msg/hour	$10	Creativity/writing
Claude 3 Opus	$25/month	100 msg/hour	$15	Document analysis
Gemini Advanced	$22/month	60 msg/hour	$12	Real-time searches
ElevenLabs API	$5/month	30,000 characters	$0.30	Realistic audio
Runway ML API	$15/month	10 min video/month	$1.50/min	AI video editing

Key **Insight**:

"For small projects: Use monthly plans. If you process >500K tokens/month, contract APIs in bulk.

Lead Magnet: "Automation Kit 2025"

Includes:

1. 10 preconfigured Zapier/IFTTT flows (importable)

2. List of affordable APIs for startups (<$50/month)

3. Video guide to creating AI videos in 5 steps

Exercise: Design Your Automation

Step 1: Choose 1 repetitive task (e.g., answering FAQs).

Step 2: Combine:

• Inbound tool (e.g., Gmail)

• AI processor (e.g., ChatGPT)

• Outbound (e.g., Google Docs)

Full example:

"When an email arrives at 'support@mycompany.com' with 'return,' generate a PDF with:

1. Return steps

2. Prefilled form

3. Send to office printer."

Financial Tips for Startups

1. Always test freemium plans before paying.

2. Combine tools: Use ChatGPT + ElevenLabs (25 total) vs. all-in-one tools (100+).

3. Negotiate annual volume discounts (save up to 30%).

List of Essential Prompts to Master AI:

Prompt Engineering Survival Pack (2025)

1. Prompts for E-Commerce

• **Product Descriptions:**

"Write a [product] description for [audience]. Highlight [emotional benefit] and [sustainable fact]. Max. 100 words, [inspirational/urgent] tone."

• **Customer Responses:**

"Generate 3 empathetic responses for a dissatisfied customer with [problem]. Include compensation (e.g., discount/free shipping)."

2. Prompts for Digital Marketing

• **LinkedIn Viral Posts:**

"Create a post on [topic] with: 1) Controversial hook, 2) 3 actionable tips, 3) Engagement question. Example tone: Gary Vee."

• **Nurturing Emails:**

"Write an email to sell [product/service] to [audience]. Use: 1) Specific pain point, 2) Impactful statistic, 3) Clear CTA. Max. 150 words."

3. Prompts for Education

• **Explaining Complex Concepts:**

"Describe [concept] to a 10-year-old. Use 1 everyday analogy and 1 visual example. Max. 5 lines."

• **Creating Quizzes:**

"Create 5 multiple-choice questions on [topic]. Include 1 case study question and answers with explanations."

4. Prompts for Business

● **Executive Reports:**

"Summarize this data in a 1-page report for CEOs. Highlight 3 key insights and 1 recommendation. Format: bullet points + suggested chart."

● **Productive Meetings:**

"Turn this transcript into: 1) 3 agreements (WHAT/WHO/WHEN), 2) 2 risks, 3) 1 innovative idea."

5. Prompts for Daily Life

● **Meal Planning:**

"Generate a weekly menu for [diet]. Include: shopping list, 30-minute prep time, and 1 quick recipe for busy days."

● **Travel Planning:**

"[X]-day itinerary in [city] for [profile]. Include: 1 cultural activity/day, 1 local restaurant, and 1 safety tip."

Bonus: Prompts for Specific Tools

MidJourney:

"[Concept] image in [artist] style. Focus: [key detail]. Color palette: [hues]. --v 6 --ar 16:9"

ElevenLabs:

"Narrate this text in a female voice, with a warm tone and dramatic pauses at [key phrases]. Speed: 90%. Export to MP3."

ChatGPT/Gemini, Claude:

"Acting as [role]. My goal is [X]. Format: [list/table]. Hue: [Y]. Avoidance: [Z]. --temperature 0.5"

Why this gift makes a difference:

● **Saves time**: Ready-to-copy/paste prompts.

- **Teaches patterns**: Each example includes "How to modify for your case."

- **Updated 2025**: Compatible with the latest AI versions.

Dear reader,

If you've made it this far, you already have the power to communicate with AI like a pro—no need to be an engineer, programmer, or tech expert.

This book isn't the end, but the first step toward a future where you'll master the most advanced tools if you just know what to ask for and how to ask for it.

Three Thoughts for Your Next Stage:

1. AI Is Your Ally, Not Your Replacement

The best results come when you combine your human creativity with the speed and precision of artificial intelligence. You provide the "what" and the "why"; AI helps you with the "how."

2. The Secret Is in Iteration

Your first prompts won't be perfect, and that's okay. Refine, adjust, and try again. Every mistake is a step closer to mastering the art of prompt engineering.

3. The Future Belongs to the Curious

The tools evolve, but the principle remains the same: whoever asks the best questions gets the best answers. Stay hungry to learn.

Your Parting Gift:

As a thank you for being part of this adventure, I'm leaving you with one last magic template (use it when you feel stuck):

"Act like an expert in [your field]. I need to solve [specific problem].

- Constraints: [clear boundaries]

- Expected format: [e.g., list, table, summary]

- Tone: [e.g., professional/fun]

Give me 3 different options for approaching this."*

What to Do Now?

Open your favorite AI tool and try a prompt from this book.

"Technology changes, but your capacity to learn is eternal. Ready for your next challenge?"

Table of Contents

Prompt Engineering for Beginners: A Non-Technical Guide to Mastering AI Tools (2025 Edition)

- Business: Quick reports, data analysis

- Daily Life: Meal planning, travel, fitness

- Downloadable templates (lead magnets)

Chapter 5: Free and Paid Tools

- Platform comparison (ChatGPT Plus vs. Gemini Advanced vs. Claude Pro)

- Useful extensions (AIPRM, WebChatGPT, Merlin)

- Special Section

o Tool-specific prompts

o AI audio/video tools (ElevenLabs, Runway ML)

o Automation with Zapier/IFTTT

o Cost comparison between APIs

Part 3: Advanced Resources

Chapter Chapter 5: Ethics and Best Practices

- Biases in AI: How to Detect and Avoid Them

- Data Privacy with Third-Party Tools

- Responsible Use in Professional Settings

Chapter 7: The Future of Prompt Engineering

- Trends 2025-2030

- How to Stay Up-to-Date

- Recommended Resources (Courses, Communities, Podcasts)

Appendices and Resources

- Appendix A: Performance Metrics (Comparative Tables)

- Appendix B: Glossary of Simplified Technical Terms

- Appendix C: Complete List of Mentioned Tools

- Bonus:

o Downloadable Template Kit (PDF + Notion)

o Access to a Private Community (Discord/WhatsApp)